Thriving on Plants: The Ultimate Guide to an Organic Vegan Lifestyle

Kevin Luna

Published by Kevin Luna, 2023.

While every precaution has been taken in the preparation of this book, the publisher assumes no responsibility for errors or omissions, or for damages resulting from the use of the information contained herein.

THRIVING ON PLANTS: THE ULTIMATE GUIDE TO AN ORGANIC VEGAN LIFESTYLE

First edition. October 27, 2023.

Copyright © 2023 Kevin Luna.

ISBN: 979-8223236603

Written by Kevin Luna.

Chapter 1: My Journey to Thriving on Plants

Welcome to the beginning of a transformative journey toward vibrant health, ethical living, and the boundless possibilities of an organic vegan lifestyle. As we set out on this path together, I want to share with you the deeply personal story that ignited my passion for embracing a plant-based existence.

The Unforeseen Turning Point

At 25 years old, my life took a sharp turn into uncharted territory. I was diagnosed with an uncommon, relentlessly painful autoimmune disease called ankylosing spondylitis. This news was a shock to my system, as I grappled with the idea that pain and discomfort would become constant companions in my daily life.

For six long years, I was entangled in a daily battle with my condition. The pursuit of relief led me down winding paths of treatments, medications, and moments of despair. But amid the darkness, a flicker of hope endured.

I was convinced that there had to be a better way, a path to healing that transcended pharmaceuticals. I yearned for a lifestyle that embraced ethical choices, nurtured the environment, and provided the healing sanctuary my body so desperately needed.

The Birth of Transformation

This conviction marked the genesis of a profound transformation, one that encompassed more than just physical healing. It encompassed a holistic shift in mindset, values, and daily practices. It started with the very core of my existence: what I chose to put on my plate.

In the pages that follow, I will unveil the knowledge and insights that guided me along this extraordinary journey. It's a voyage centered on the captivating world of whole foods, the rejuvenating spirit of a vegan lifestyle, and the importance of nurturing not just your body, but your mind and the planet we call home.

I learned that the key to my recovery was mending my gut, healing the damage, and fostering a healthier, more robust immune system. It became evident that the food I consumed was not mere sustenance but a powerful form of medicine for my body and soul. The adoption of an organic, plant-based diet breathed life into me, and I am living proof that this path is not only life-affirming but life-changing.

As we traverse this book together, you'll be empowered with the knowledge of how a holistic, vegan, and organic lifestyle can play a pivotal role in managing and even reversing the symptoms of autoimmune diseases like ankylosing spondylitis. The journey may be challenging at times, but it's one filled with profound rewards and boundless opportunities for growth and well-being.

Welcome to the commencement of your own transformation, where you have the potential to unlock the secrets to optimal health, a compassionate existence, and the delectable flavors of whole foods. The journey to thriving on plants begins now, and I am honored to be your guide.

Chapter 2: The Wonders of a Plant-Based Lifestyle: Nourishing Body, Mind, and Planet

As we delve further into the realm of a plant-based lifestyle, it's essential to grasp the fundamental principles that underpin this transformative journey. In this chapter, we will explore the captivating world of plant-based living, the significance of soil health, and the importance of nutrient-dense foods. We'll understand why it's not just a dietary choice but a profound lifestyle shift that can influence our health, ethics, and our planet.

The Heart of Plant-Based Living

At its core, a plant-based lifestyle revolves around a simple, yet revolutionary idea: embracing a diet primarily composed of foods derived from plants. This means vegetables, fruits, legumes, whole grains, nuts, and seeds become the stars of your culinary repertoire. Such a dietary shift can offer profound benefits to your overall well-being, and we'll uncover these benefits in detail throughout this book.

Nourishing Your Body and Mind

The foods you consume are more than just fuel; they are building blocks for your body's intricate machinery. A plant-based diet brims with an abundance of essential nutrients, antioxidants, vitamins, and minerals that can energize your body, reduce inflammation, and boost your immune system. This is the foundation of our quest for optimal health.

Furthermore, the nutrient density of plant-based foods is a crucial aspect of this lifestyle. Nutrient-dense foods provide an abundance of vitamins and minerals relative to their caloric content. They're like little powerhouses of nutrition, and they are abundant in a plant-based diet. These foods not only fuel your body but also promote vibrant health.

The Ethical Choice

Choosing a plant-based lifestyle isn't just about personal health; it's also an ethical statement. It signifies a commitment to compassion, both for the animals that share our planet and for the environment. By reducing or eliminating animal products from our diets, we participate in the global movement to decrease animal suffering and lower our carbon footprint.

Healing the Planet

The impact of our dietary choices extends far beyond our individual lives. The cultivation and production of plant-based foods are generally more sustainable and environmentally friendly than animal agriculture. When we opt for a plant-based lifestyle, we contribute to the reduction of deforestation, greenhouse gas emissions, and the conservation of vital resources like water and land.

The Soil Connection

Soil health is a linchpin in the plant-based lifestyle. Healthy, fertile soil teeming with microorganisms provides the foundation for nutrient-dense crops. When we choose plant-based foods, we promote sustainable agriculture practices that prioritize soil health. The nutrients and minerals drawn from rich, well-nourished soil find their way into our meals, offering us unparalleled nourishment.

A Delectable Adventure

One common misconception about plant-based living is that it's restrictive or lacks flavor. In reality, this lifestyle opens the door to a world of culinary creativity. You'll be amazed by the variety and vibrancy of plant-based dishes. Whether you're a seasoned chef or a beginner in the kitchen, you'll find that embracing plant-based cuisine is a delectable adventure.

As we continue our exploration of this lifestyle, we'll delve into practical tips and mouthwatering recipes that will not only nourish your body but also tantalize your taste buds. The path to thriving on plants is a sensory journey, a celebration of life, well-being, and the interconnected health of the planet.

So, as we step into this verdant world of plant-based living, prepare to embark on a transformative odyssey. The next chapters will guide you through the science, the principles, and the delectable possibilities of this way of life. Your journey has just begun, and the rewards awaiting you are nothing short of extraordinary.

Chapter 3: Cultivating Nutrient-Dense Foods for Health and Gut Renewal

As we navigate the world of plant-based living, it's essential to understand the profound significance of nutrient-dense foods and how they contribute to your overall health and well-being, including the incredible contributions of leafy greens, vibrant berries, and a wide array of plant-based foods. In this chapter, we'll delve into the concept of nutrient density, the role of antioxidants in combating oxidative stress, and how these foods can promote gut health, a key factor in your overall well-being.

The Power of Nutrient Density

Nutrient density refers to the concentration of essential nutrients within a given portion of food. These essential nutrients include vitamins, minerals, antioxidants, and phytochemicals that promote health and vitality. When you consume nutrient-dense foods, you provide your body with an abundance of these critical elements relative to the number of calories.

For individuals embracing a plant-based lifestyle, nutrient-dense foods are the cornerstone of a healthy diet. They offer a vast array of health benefits, including improved energy levels, a strengthened immune system, and the ability to fend off chronic diseases. Consuming nutrient-dense foods is not just about sustaining life; it's about thriving.

The Rainbow on Your Plate: A Symphony of Plant-Based Foods

In the world of plant-based living, the choices are as diverse as the colors of the rainbow. Let's explore the captivating contributions of a variety of nutrient-dense plant-based foods and how they can benefit your health and gut:

- **Leafy Greens:** Spinach, kale, Swiss chard, and collard greens are nutritional powerhouses. Rich in vitamins A, C, and K, as well as minerals like iron and calcium, they support bone health and boost the immune system. These greens are potent sources of antioxidants that combat inflammation and protect your cells. 90 Recipes in the end incorporate many leafy greens. I recommend adding "Green Spectrum" to your daily use to get high quality nutrient dense greens from the land and sea. Green Spectrum[1] use gift code EMPATHY for a discount.

Spirulina and Chlorella: These blue-green algae are packed with nutrients, including protein, vitamins, and minerals. Spirulina is a source of gamma-linolenic acid (GLA), a beneficial fatty acid, while chlorella is renowned for its detoxifying properties. They're excellent additions to smoothies and can provide a nutritional punch to your diet. The cleanest and most nutrient dense source of Spirulina can be found here Spirulina[2] and the best cracked cell chlorella that has never been heat treated and hand pressed, no machines, and sound frequency to crack the cell wall can be found here Chlorella[3] use gift code EMPATHY for a discount.

---

1. https://ishoppurium.com/AllProducts/2402

2. https://ishoppurium.com/AllProducts/2432%20

3. https://ishoppurium.com/AllProducts/2483

- **Berries:** Blueberries, strawberries, raspberries, blackberries, and other dark berries offer a cornucopia of antioxidants, vitamins, and minerals. They support brain health, promote heart health, and bolster your immune system. These fruits are not only delicious but also combat oxidative stress, which can lead to chronic diseases. I recommend adding Bio Fruit[4] as it has the best variety of all these berries and more of the most nutrient dense fruits on the planet, use gift code EMPATHY for a discount.

- **Legumes:** Beans, lentils, and peas are excellent sources of protein, fiber, and essential minerals like potassium and magnesium. They support digestive health and provide sustained energy while keeping your gut flora happy.

- **Nuts and Seeds:** Almonds, chia seeds, flaxseeds, and walnuts are dense with healthy fats, fiber, and essential nutrients like vitamin E, omega-3 fatty acids, and phytochemicals. They promote heart health, provide sustained energy, and benefit gut health.

- **Cruciferous Vegetables:** Broccoli, cauliflower, Brussels sprouts, and cabbage are renowned for their cancer-fighting properties. They're rich in vitamins, minerals, and phytonutrients that support gut health and overall well-being.

The Role of Antioxidants

Antioxidants are your body's defenders against oxidative stress and the damage caused by free radicals. Plant-based foods, particularly those rich in colorful compounds like carotenoids, flavonoids, and polyphenols, are replete with antioxidants. These compounds help to protect your cells, reduce inflammation, and combat chronic diseases.

Nurturing Gut Health

Your gut is a bustling ecosystem of trillions of microorganisms. A diet rich in fiber from fruits, vegetables, and whole grains provides nourishment to the beneficial bacteria in your gut. These

---

4. https://ishoppurium.com/AllProducts/2491

microorganisms play a pivotal role in digestion, nutrient absorption, and the synthesis of essential vitamins.

Additionally, foods like fermented products (such as sauerkraut, kimchi, and kombucha) are excellent sources of probiotics, which contribute to a balanced gut flora. A healthy gut is not only essential for efficient digestion but also for overall well-being, as it is intricately linked to your immune system, brain health, and even mood.

Incorporating Nutrient-Dense Foods into Your Diet

To enjoy the myriad benefits of nutrient-dense plant-based foods, aim to fill your plate with an array of colors and food groups. Seek out locally grown, organic produce whenever possible, as these foods often boast superior nutrient content due to sustainable farming practices. Incorporate them into your meals, snacks, and drinks to nourish your body from the inside out.

In the chapters that follow, we'll delve into practical tips and mouthwatering recipes that will help you harness the power of these nutrient-dense plant-based foods while supporting your gut health and enhancing your overall well-being. Your journey to thriving on plants is not just about what you exclude from your diet; it's about what you embrace, savor, and celebrate. Each bite is an investment in your health, and the rewards are boundless.

So, as we continue on this path, prepare to awaken your taste buds and nourish your body with the abundant riches of nutrient-dense plant foods, all while cultivating a thriving gut. Your journey to optimal health and vitality has only just begun, with a vibrant

Chapter 4: Thriving with Plants at Any Age: Lessons from Research and Living Proof

In our journey toward embracing a plant-based lifestyle, it's essential to recognize that age is not a barrier to thriving on plants. In this chapter, we'll explore the remarkable findings of scientific research supporting the benefits of plant-based living at every stage of life. We'll also draw inspiration from individuals who have not only excelled but have thrived on this path, including renowned athletes like Novak Djokovic.

A Lifelong Adventure: The Research Perspective

The idea that a plant-based lifestyle can support health and vitality throughout one's life is not a mere belief; it's supported by a growing body of scientific research. Here are some key insights from recent studies:

- **Longevity:** Research suggests that plant-based diets are associated with a lower risk of chronic diseases and may contribute to a longer life. A study published in the Journal of the American Heart Association in 2021 found that individuals who followed plant-based diets had a 10% lower risk of developing heart disease compared to those with non-plant-based diets.

- **Cognitive Health:** Plant-based diets, rich in antioxidants and anti-inflammatory compounds, may support brain health. A study published in the journal Neurology in 2020 reported that individuals who consumed a plant-based diet had a lower risk of cognitive impairment and dementia.

- **Bone Health:** Contrary to concerns about calcium intake, plant-based diets can provide sufficient calcium for bone health. A study published in the journal Nutrients in 2018 found that plant-based sources of calcium, like leafy greens and fortified plant milks, can promote bone health without the drawbacks of animal-derived sources.

- **Athletic Performance:** Elite athletes like Novak Djokovic have demonstrated that a plant-based diet can not only sustain but enhance athletic performance. Djokovic, a tennis superstar, adopted a plant-based diet in 2011 and has since achieved numerous victories, including Grand Slam titles. His diet, rich in organic superfoods, fruits, and green juices, is credited with boosting his endurance and recovery.

Living Proof: Athletes Thriving on Plants

Novak Djokovic is an inspiring example of an athlete thriving on a plant-based diet. A significant portion of his diet consists of organic superfoods, fruits, and organic green juices. These choices provide him with a wealth of antioxidants, vitamins, and minerals that support his physical and mental resilience. Djokovic's diet is tailored to fuel his athletic demands and optimize his performance on the tennis court.

His journey showcases that a plant-based lifestyle can not only maintain but enhance athletic performance. From superfoods like spirulina and chlorella to the vibrant nutrients in organic fruits, his choices emphasize the power of plant-based nutrition in boosting endurance and recovery. Djokovic's experiences challenge the myth that animal products are necessary for athletic success.

Thriving at Any Age

Whether you're in your 20s, 50s, or beyond, a plant-based lifestyle can empower you to thrive at any age. The research and living proof of top athletes like Djokovic demonstrate that this way of living offers a fountain of youth for your health, vitality, and well-being.

As we journey deeper into this book, we'll explore practical tips and inspiring stories that will help you transition to and embrace a plant-based lifestyle at any age. The power to thrive with plants is not bound by time or circumstance; it's a choice you can make today for a brighter, healthier tomorrow.

Let's continue forward with confidence, inspired by the research and stories of individuals who have embraced plant-based living and experienced its profound benefits. Your journey to thriving on plants is a lifelong adventure, and it's one filled with boundless potential and vibrant health.

Chapter 5: Building Strength and Longevity with Plant-Based Nutrition

In this chapter, we'll explore the intriguing world of plant-based strength and longevity, with a particular focus on vegan bodybuilders who have shattered stereotypes and defied expectations. We'll also delve into the unsettling reality that many bodybuilders, despite their formidable strength, succumb to heart disease and how a plant-based lifestyle offers a path to a heart-healthy, vibrant life.

Vegan Bodybuilders: Breaking Stereotypes

The world of bodybuilding is often associated with images of massive athletes consuming vast quantities of animal products to gain muscle mass. However, there's a growing wave of vegan bodybuilders who are changing this narrative. These individuals have not only built impressive physiques but have also shattered stereotypes surrounding plant-based nutrition.

Names like Patrik Baboumian, Torre Washington, and Nimai Delgado have emerged as vegan bodybuilding icons. They attribute their strength, endurance, and recovery to a plant-based diet rich in legumes, grains, fruits, and vegetables. Their stories challenge the notion that animal products are the exclusive key to building muscle and strength.

Heart Health and Bodybuilding

Despite their muscular appearances, some bodybuilders face an unsettling reality: heart disease is a prevalent risk in the world of bodybuilding. The emphasis on high-protein, animal-based diets, often loaded with saturated fats and cholesterol, can lead to a higher likelihood of heart issues, including heart attacks.

The combination of intense workouts, extreme protein consumption, and the use of supplements can create a perfect storm for heart-related problems. The paradox of strong bodies succumbing to heart disease underscores the importance of dietary choices, even for those engaged in intense physical training.

Longevity and Plant-Based Nutrition

In contrast, plant-based nutrition offers an avenue for longevity and heart health. Research has consistently shown that plant-based diets, rich in whole foods and devoid of animal products, can reduce the risk of heart disease. These diets are associated with lower blood pressure, improved cholesterol profiles, and decreased inflammation - all critical factors for a healthy heart.

A landmark study published in the Journal of the American Heart Association in 2019 demonstrated that a plant-based diet can reduce the risk of heart failure. The study revealed that those who adhered to a plant-based diet had a 42% lower risk of developing heart failure compared to those who did not.

Thriving with Plant-Based Strength and Health

The stories of vegan bodybuilders who have defied stereotypes, coupled with the research on heart health and longevity, underscore the power of a plant-based lifestyle. Whether you're seeking to build strength, enhance your cardiovascular health, or enjoy a longer, healthier life, plant-based nutrition offers a compelling path forward.

In the chapters that follow, we'll delve into practical guidance and success stories that will inspire you to embrace the strength and longevity that a plant-based lifestyle can offer. Your journey to thriving on plants is not just about building muscle; it's about nurturing a strong heart and experiencing a vibrant, robust life.

Let's continue forward, drawing motivation from vegan bodybuilders who have risen to the pinnacle of strength while prioritizing heart health and longevity. Your journey to thriving on plants is filled with opportunities for physical vitality and enduring well-being.

Chapter 6: Harnessing the Healing Power of Plant-Based Foods

In this chapter, we will explore the remarkable healing potential of plant-based nutrition. We'll delve into the science of how plant-based foods can combat chronic diseases and enhance your overall well-being. From diabetes management to cancer prevention, we'll uncover how your diet can be a powerful tool for healing and thriving.

Plant-Based Foods as Medicine

The concept of food as medicine is not new, but it's gaining renewed attention in the world of healthcare. Plant-based nutrition is at the forefront of this movement, and for good reason. The abundance of antioxidants, vitamins, minerals, and phytonutrients in plant-based foods makes them powerful allies in preventing and managing chronic diseases.

- **Diabetes Management:** Research has shown that a plant-based diet can be a game-changer for individuals with diabetes. A study published in the Journal of the American College of Nutrition in 2020 found that a plant-based diet improved blood sugar control and reduced the need for diabetes medications.

- **Heart Health:** The American Heart Association has recognized the heart-healthy benefits of plant-based diets. Consuming more fruits, vegetables, whole grains, and legumes can reduce the risk of heart disease. These foods help lower blood pressure, improve cholesterol levels, and decrease inflammation.

- **Cancer Prevention:** A diet rich in plant-based foods is associated with a reduced risk of certain types of cancer. The American Cancer Society emphasizes the importance of vegetables, fruits, and whole grains in cancer prevention due to their high fiber, antioxidant, and anti-inflammatory content.

- **Gut Health:** The role of the gut microbiome in overall health is an area of growing research. Plant-based diets, with their abundant fiber and prebiotics, support a diverse and beneficial gut microbiota. A healthy gut is linked to a strong immune system, improved digestion, and even mental well-being.

Real-Life Healing Stories

Throughout this chapter, we'll also share inspiring real-life stories of individuals who have harnessed the healing power of plant-based nutrition to overcome chronic diseases. From managing autoimmune conditions to reversing heart disease, their experiences serve as living proof that a plant-based lifestyle can be transformative.

Your Journey to Healing and Thriving

As we continue to explore the healing potential of plant-based foods, you'll gain valuable insights into how dietary choices can impact your health and well-being. Your journey to thriving on plants is not just about prevention; it's about healing and rejuvenating your body from within.

In the chapters that follow, we'll delve into practical advice and delicious recipes that will empower you to harness the healing power of plant-based nutrition in your own life. Your path to vibrant health and well-being is marked by the choices you make, and the rewards are immeasurable.

Chapter 7: The Joy of Plant-Based Cooking

In this chapter, we'll embark on a culinary journey that celebrates the art of plant-based cooking. We'll explore the diverse flavors, textures, and aromas that make plant-based cuisine not just a dietary choice but a delightful adventure for your taste buds. From the magic of spices to the beauty of seasonal produce, you'll discover the joy of crafting delicious, satisfying meals that promote your health and well-being.

The Pleasures of Plant-Based Ingredients

Plant-based cooking is an exploration of the abundance of ingredients that nature provides. From crisp, colorful vegetables to hearty grains and legumes, the plant kingdom offers a palette of flavors and textures to create dishes that nourish your body and soul.

- **Spices and Herbs:** The world of spices and herbs is a treasure trove of culinary possibilities. They not only enhance the taste of your dishes but also provide health benefits. From turmeric's anti-inflammatory properties to the immune-boosting qualities of garlic and ginger, these flavorful additions elevate your meals.

- **Seasonal Produce:** Embracing seasonal fruits and vegetables not only connects you with the cycles of nature but also ensures the freshness and flavor of your dishes. You'll learn the joys of incorporating seasonal delights into your cooking, from the sweetness of summer berries to the earthiness of autumn squashes.

- **Whole Grains:** Whole grains like quinoa, brown rice, and oats are staples of plant-based cuisine. They provide sustained energy, dietary fiber, and a rich, nutty taste to your meals. Discover how to make these grains the foundation of a hearty, satisfying dish.

- **Nuts and Seeds:** Almonds, walnuts, chia seeds, and flaxseeds are not only great for snacking but also fantastic additions to your recipes. They provide healthy fats, protein, and a delightful crunch that adds depth and texture to your dishes.

The Art of Plant-Based Cooking

Plant-based cooking is more than just assembling ingredients; it's an art form. You'll learn to create vibrant, satisfying meals that rival their animal-based counterparts. Whether you're a seasoned chef or a novice in the kitchen, you'll find that plant-based cuisine offers endless opportunities for creativity and culinary exploration.

As we delve into the world of plant-based cooking, you'll gain practical tips, step-by-step recipes, and guidance to craft a diverse array of delicious meals. From breakfast to dinner, snacks to desserts, your plant-based kitchen will become a hub of culinary innovation and a source of joy for you and your loved ones.

Chapter 8: Your 90 Organic Vegan Recipes

In this final chapter, we present the culmination of our plant-based journey: a collection of 90 delectable organic vegan recipes that showcase the diverse and mouthwatering possibilities of this lifestyle. These recipes cover a wide range of dishes, from breakfast to dinner, snacks, and desserts. Each recipe is crafted to nourish your body with nutrient-dense ingredients while satisfying your taste buds with a symphony of flavors.

From hearty and wholesome soups to colorful salads bursting with freshness, from comforting pasta dishes to innovative plant-based burgers, your culinary adventure awaits. You'll also find sweet indulgences like dairy-free ice creams, fruit-infused desserts, and guilt-free treats that prove you can have your cake and eat it too.

With these 90 organic vegan recipes, you'll have the tools and inspiration to enjoy plant-based cuisine to the fullest. Whether you're looking to create a feast for friends and family or prepare a quick, nutritious meal for yourself, these recipes will become your trusted companions in the kitchen.

Your journey to thriving on plants is not only a path to optimal health but also an invitation to savor the joys of plant-based cooking. As you explore these recipes, may you find the inspiration and motivation to embrace a vibrant, fulfilling, and nourishing plant-based lifestyle that will transform your life for the better. Bon appétit!

The best piece of advice I could possibly give you is this right here.

he 90 Day Ultimate Lifestyle Transformation is the best tool at your disposal to felling, looking and performing your best.

As my special Reward and treat to you for making it to the end of this book, I am gifting you $120 off the Ultimate Lifestyle Transformation, 0 tax, free shipping, and a free portable blender! Use this link to purchase now and choose any of these 90 recipes to pair with your 90 day Transformation!

https://www.ultlifestyle.com?giftcard=emp

Here is my Free Support Group that everyone is invite to https://www.facebook.com/groups/veganwellnesstribe/

Here are the first 10 organic vegan recipes that kickstart your Ultimate Lifestyle Transformation for 90 days. These recipes are not only delicious but also simple to prepare, making it easy to maintain your plant-based journey.

Recipe 1: Energizing Green Smoothie

Ingredients:

- 1 cup organic spinach

- 1 cup organic kale

- 1 organic banana

- 1 cup organic almond milk
- 1 tbsp organic chia seeds
- 1 tsp organic spirulina (Use Gift code EMPATHY for discount[1])
- 2 tbsp organic Power Shake (Use Gift code EMPATHY for discount[2])

Instructions:

1. Blend spinach, kale, banana, and almond milk until smooth.

2. Add chia seeds and spirulina, blend again.

3. Sweeten with organic Agave if desired.

4. Serve and start your day with a burst of energy.

Recipe 2: Quinoa and Black Bean Salad

Ingredients:

- 1 cup organic quinoa
- 1 can (15 oz) organic black beans, drained and rinsed
- 1 cup organic cherry tomatoes, halved
- 1/2 cup organic red onion, finely chopped
- 1/4 cup organic cilantro, chopped
- 2 tbsp organic lime juice
- 2 tbsp organic olive oil
- Salt and pepper to taste

Instructions:

1. Cook quinoa according to package instructions and let it cool.

2. In a large bowl, combine quinoa, black beans, cherry tomatoes, red onion, and cilantro.

3. In a small bowl, whisk together lime juice, olive oil, salt, and pepper.

4. Pour the dressing over the salad and toss to combine.

5. Chill in the refrigerator before serving.

Recipe 3: Creamy Avocado Pasta

Ingredients:

---

1.   https://ishoppurium.com/AllProducts/2432

2.   https://ishoppurium.com/AllProducts/2001

- 8 oz organic whole-grain pasta
- 2 organic avocados
- 1 organic lemon, juiced
- 2 cloves organic garlic
- 1/4 cup organic basil leaves
- 2 tbsp organic olive oil
- Salt and pepper to taste

Instructions:

1. Cook pasta according to package instructions and set aside.

2. In a food processor, blend avocados, lemon juice, garlic, basil, and olive oil until smooth.

3. Season with salt and pepper.

4. Toss the creamy avocado sauce with cooked pasta.

5. Serve with a sprinkle of fresh basil.

Recipe 4: Roasted Vegetable Buddha Bowl

Ingredients:

- 1 cup organic sweet potatoes, cubed
- 1 cup organic broccoli florets
- 1 cup organic carrots, sliced
- 1 cup organic chickpeas, drained and rinsed
- 2 tbsp organic olive oil
- 1 tsp organic cumin
- 1 tsp organic paprika
- Salt and pepper to taste
- 2 cups cooked organic quinoa
- 1/4 cup organic hummus
- 1/4 cup organic tahini sauce

Instructions:

1. Preheat the oven to 400°F (200°C).

2. In a bowl, toss sweet potatoes, broccoli, carrots, and chickpeas with olive oil, cumin, paprika, salt, and pepper.

3. Spread the vegetables on a baking sheet and roast for 25-30 minutes or until tender.

4. To assemble the Buddha bowl, start with cooked quinoa, add the roasted vegetables, and drizzle with hummus and tahini sauce.

5. Enjoy the flavors and textures in every bite.

Recipe 5: Chickpea and Vegetable Curry

Ingredients:

- 1 tbsp organic coconut oil

- 1 organic onion, chopped

- 2 cloves organic garlic, minced

- 1 organic bell pepper, diced

- 1 cup organic cauliflower florets

- 1 cup organic carrots, sliced

- 2 tbsp organic curry powder

- 1 can (15 oz) organic chickpeas, drained and rinsed

- 1 can (15 oz) organic diced tomatoes

- 1 can (15 oz) organic coconut milk

- Salt and pepper to taste

Instructions:

1. In a large pot, heat coconut oil over medium heat.

2. Add onion and garlic and sauté until fragrant.

3. Stir in bell pepper, cauliflower, and carrots, and cook for a few minutes.

4. Add curry powder and cook for another minute.

5. Add chickpeas, diced tomatoes, and coconut milk.

6. Bring to a boil, reduce heat, and simmer for 20-25 minutes.

7. Season with salt and pepper.

8. Serve with rice or quinoa.

Recipe 6: Spaghetti Aglio e Olio with Cherry Tomatoes

Ingredients:

- 8 oz organic whole-grain spaghetti

- 4 cloves organic garlic, thinly sliced

- 1/4 cup organic olive oil
- 1 cup organic cherry tomatoes, halved
- 1/4 cup organic fresh basil, chopped
- Red pepper flakes (optional)
- Salt and pepper to taste

Instructions:

1. Cook spaghetti according to package instructions and set aside.

2. In a large skillet, heat olive oil over medium heat.

3. Add sliced garlic and sauté until fragrant.

4. Add cherry tomatoes and cook for a few minutes until they start to soften.

5. Toss in cooked spaghetti and fresh basil. Stir to combine.

6. Season with red pepper flakes (if desired), salt, and pepper.

7. Serve with an extra drizzle of olive oil.

Recipe 7: Rainbow Chopped Salad with Lemon-Tahini Dressing

Ingredients:

- 4 cups organic mixed greens
- 1 cup organic red cabbage, finely chopped
- 1 cup organic carrots, grated
- 1 cup organic bell peppers, diced
- 1 cup organic cucumber, diced
- 1 cup organic cherry tomatoes, halved
- 1/4 cup organic red onion, finely chopped
- 1/4 cup organic fresh parsley, chopped

For the Lemon-Tahini Dressing:

- 3 tbsp organic tahini

- 2 tbsp organic lemon juice
- 1 tbsp organic olive oil
- 1 clove organic garlic, minced
- Water to thin

- Salt and pepper to taste

Instructions:

1. In a large bowl, combine mixed greens, red cabbage, carrots, bell peppers, cucumber, cherry tomatoes, red onion, and parsley.

2. In a separate bowl, whisk together tahini, lemon juice, olive oil, garlic, and water until desired consistency is reached.

3. Season the dressing with salt and pepper.

4. Drizzle the salad with the lemon-tahini dressing just before serving.

Recipe 8: Vegan Lentil and Sweet Potato Stew

Ingredients:

- 1 tbsp organic olive oil
- 1 organic onion, chopped
- 2 cloves organic garlic, minced
- 1 organic sweet potato, peeled and diced
- 1 cup organic brown or green lentils
- 4 cups organic vegetable broth
- 1 can (15 oz) organic diced tomatoes
- 2 tsp organic ground cumin
- 1 tsp organic ground coriander
- 1/2 tsp organic smoked paprika
- Salt and pepper to taste
- 4 cups organic kale, chopped

Instructions:

1. In a large pot, heat olive oil over medium heat.

2. Add onion and garlic and sauté until fragrant.

3. Stir in sweet potato, lentils, vegetable broth, diced tomatoes, cumin, coriander, smoked paprika, salt, and pepper.

4. Bring to a boil, reduce heat, and simmer for 25-30 minutes or until lentils and sweet potatoes are tender.

5. Stir in chopped kale and cook for a few more minutes until wilted.

6. Serve the hearty stew for a satisfying meal.

Recipe 9: Vegan Chickpea and Vegetable Stir-Fry
Ingredients:
- 2 cups organic broccoli florets
- 1 cup organic bell peppers, sliced
- 1 cup organic snap peas
- 1 cup organic carrots, sliced
- 1 cup organic mushrooms, sliced
- 1 can (15 oz) organic chickpeas, drained and rinsed
- 3 tbsp organic low-sodium soy sauce or tamari
- 2 tbsp organic hoisin sauce
- 1 tbsp organic sesame oil
- 2 cloves organic garlic, minced
- 1 tsp organic ginger, minced
- Cooked organic brown rice or quinoa for serving
Instructions:
1. In a large skillet or wok, heat sesame oil over medium-high heat.
2. Add broccoli, bell peppers, snap peas, carrots, and mushrooms. Stir-fry until the vegetables are tender-crisp.
3. Stir in chickpeas, garlic, and ginger.
4. In a small bowl, whisk together soy sauce or tamari and hoisin sauce.
5. Pour the sauce over the stir-fry and toss to coat the vegetables and chickpeas.
6. Serve over cooked brown rice or quinoa.
Recipe 10: Vegan Avocado Chocolate Mousse
Ingredients:
- 2 ripe organic avocados
- 1/4 cup organic unsweetened cocoa powder
- 1/4 cup organic maple syrup or agave nectar
- 1 tsp organic vanilla extract
- A pinch of salt
- Fresh organic berries for topping (e.g., strawberries, raspberries)

Instructions:

1. Scoop the flesh of the avocados into a food processor.

2. Add cocoa powder, maple syrup or agave nectar, vanilla extract, and a pinch of salt.

3. Blend until smooth and creamy.

4. Chill the mousse in the refrigerator for at least 30 minutes.

5. Serve with fresh organic berries on top for a delightful, guilt-free dessert.

These first 10 organic vegan recipes are a delicious and nutritious start to your 90-day Ultimate Lifestyle Transformation. As you progress through the remaining 80 recipes, you'll continue to discover a world of flavors, nourishment, and culinary creativity that will support your plant-based journey and help you thrive for the long term. Enjoy!

Recipe 11: Mediterranean Quinoa Salad

Ingredients:

- 1 cup organic quinoa
- 1 can (15 oz) organic chickpeas, drained and rinsed
- 1 cup organic cucumber, diced
- 1 cup organic cherry tomatoes, halved
- 1/4 cup organic red onion, finely chopped
- 1/4 cup organic Kalamata olives, pitted and sliced
- 1/4 cup organic fresh parsley, chopped
- 3 tbsp organic extra-virgin olive oil
- 2 tbsp organic lemon juice
- 1 tsp organic dried oregano
- Salt and pepper to taste

Instructions:

1. Cook quinoa according to package instructions and let it cool.

2. In a large bowl, combine quinoa, chickpeas, cucumber, cherry tomatoes, red onion, olives, and parsley.

3. In a small bowl, whisk together olive oil, lemon juice, dried oregano, salt, and pepper.

4. Pour the dressing over the salad and toss to combine.

5. Chill in the refrigerator before serving.

Recipe 12: Vegan Lentil Shepherd's Pie

Ingredients:

For the Mashed Potato Topping:

- 4 cups organic potatoes, peeled and diced

- 1/2 cup organic unsweetened almond milk

- 2 tbsp organic vegan butter

- Salt and pepper to taste

For the Lentil Filling:

- 1 cup organic brown or green lentils

- 4 cups organic vegetable broth

- 1 tbsp organic olive oil

- 1 organic onion, chopped

- 2 cloves organic garlic, minced

- 2 organic carrots, diced

- 1 cup organic peas (fresh or frozen)

- 1 tsp organic dried thyme

- Salt and pepper to taste

Instructions:

For the Mashed Potato Topping:

1. Boil potatoes until tender, then drain.

2. Mash the potatoes, adding almond milk, vegan butter, salt, and pepper. Set aside.

For the Lentil Filling:

1. In a large pot, cook lentils in vegetable broth until tender. Drain and set aside.

2. In a separate skillet, heat olive oil over medium heat.

3. Sauté onion and garlic until fragrant.

4. Add carrots, peas, dried thyme, salt, and pepper, and cook until the vegetables are tender.

5. Stir in cooked lentils.

6. Preheat your oven to 375°F (190°C).

7. In a baking dish, spread the lentil filling and top with mashed potatoes.

8. Bake for 20-25 minutes or until the top is golden.

Recipe 13: Vegan Pad Thai

Ingredients:

- 8 oz organic rice noodles

- 2 tbsp organic vegetable oil

- 1 organic red bell pepper, thinly sliced

- 1 organic carrot, julienned

- 2 cups organic broccoli florets

- 1 cup organic snap peas

- 1 cup organic firm tofu, cubed

- 2 cloves organic garlic, minced

- 1/4 cup organic tamari or soy sauce

- 2 tbsp organic maple syrup

- 2 tbsp organic lime juice

- 1 tsp organic sriracha sauce (adjust to your spice preference)

- Chopped organic peanuts and fresh cilantro for garnish

Instructions:

1. Cook rice noodles according to package instructions and set aside.

2. In a large wok or skillet, heat vegetable oil over medium-high heat.

3. Add red bell pepper, carrot, broccoli, snap peas, and tofu. Stir-fry until the vegetables are tender and tofu is slightly crispy.

4. In a small bowl, whisk together garlic, tamari or soy sauce, maple syrup, lime juice, and sriracha sauce.

5. Add cooked noodles and the sauce to the wok. Toss to combine and heat through.

6. Serve with chopped peanuts and fresh cilantro.

Recipe 14: Vegan Stuffed Bell Peppers

Ingredients:

- 4 organic bell peppers

- 1 cup organic quinoa
- 2 cups organic vegetable broth
- 1 tbsp organic olive oil
- 1 organic onion, chopped
- 2 cloves organic garlic, minced
- 1 cup organic zucchini, diced
- 1 cup organic mushrooms, diced
- 1 can (15 oz) organic black beans, drained and rinsed
- 1 cup organic diced tomatoes
- 1 tsp organic chili powder
- 1 tsp organic cumin
- Salt and pepper to taste
- 1 cup organic tomato sauce

Instructions:

1. Preheat your oven to 375°F (190°C).

2. Cut the tops off the bell peppers and remove the seeds. Set aside.

3. In a large pot, bring vegetable broth to a boil and add quinoa. Cook until the quinoa is fluffy and the broth is absorbed.

4. In a skillet, heat olive oil over medium heat. Sauté onion and garlic until fragrant.

5. Stir in zucchini and mushrooms and cook until tender.

6. Add cooked quinoa, black beans, diced tomatoes, chili powder, cumin, salt, and pepper. Mix well.

7. Stuff the bell peppers with the quinoa and vegetable mixture.

8. Place the stuffed peppers in a baking dish and pour tomato sauce over them.

9. Cover with aluminum foil and bake for 25-30 minutes.

Recipe 15: Vegan Chickpea Tikka Masala

Ingredients:

- 1 tbsp organic vegetable oil
- 1 organic onion, chopped
- 3 cloves organic garlic, minced

- 1 tbsp organic ginger, minced
- 2 tbsp organic tomato paste
- 1 can (15 oz) organic chickpeas, drained and rinsed
- 1 can (15 oz) organic diced tomatoes
- 1 cup organic coconut milk
- 2 tsp organic garam masala
- 1 tsp organic ground cumin
- 1 tsp organic ground coriander
- 1/2 tsp organic turmeric
- 1/2 tsp organic paprika
- Salt and pepper to taste
- Chopped organic cilantro for garnish

Instructions:

1. In a large skillet, heat vegetable oil over medium heat.

2. Sauté onion, garlic, and ginger until fragrant.

3. Stir in tomato paste, chickpeas, diced tomatoes, coconut milk, garam masala, cumin, coriander, turmeric, paprika, salt, and pepper.

4. Bring to a simmer and cook for 20-25 minutes, stirring occasionally.

5. Garnish with chopped cilantro and serve over rice or with naan bread.

Recipe 16: Vegan Spinach and Mushroom Stuffed Portobello Mushrooms

Ingredients:

- 4 large organic portobello mushrooms
- 1 tbsp organic olive oil
- 1 organic onion, chopped
- 2 cloves organic garlic, minced
- 2 cups organic baby spinach
- 1 cup organic mushrooms, finely chopped
- 1/2 cup organic vegan cream cheese
- 1/4 cup

organic breadcrumbs

- 1/4 cup organic vegan Parmesan cheese (optional)

- Salt and pepper to taste

Instructions:

1. Preheat your oven to 375°F (190°C).

2. Remove the stems from the portobello mushrooms and set aside.

3. In a large skillet, heat olive oil over medium heat.

4. Sauté onion and garlic until fragrant.

5. Add baby spinach and mushrooms, and cook until they are wilted and tender.

6. In a bowl, combine the sautéed mixture with vegan cream cheese, breadcrumbs, and vegan Parmesan cheese (if using). Season with salt and pepper.

7. Stuff the portobello mushrooms with the mixture.

8. Place the stuffed mushrooms in a baking dish and bake for 20-25 minutes.

Recipe 17: Vegan Butternut Squash and Red Lentil Soup

Ingredients:

- 1 organic butternut squash, peeled and cubed

- 1 cup organic red lentils

- 1 organic onion, chopped

- 2 cloves organic garlic, minced

- 1 tsp organic ground cumin

- 1 tsp organic ground coriander

- 1/2 tsp organic ground turmeric

- 1/2 tsp organic ground ginger

- 4 cups organic vegetable broth

- Salt and pepper to taste

Instructions:

1. In a large pot, combine butternut squash, red lentils, onion, garlic, cumin, coriander, turmeric, ginger, vegetable broth, salt, and pepper.

2. Bring to a boil, then reduce heat and simmer for 20-25 minutes or until the squash and lentils are tender.

3. Use an immersion blender to purée the soup until smooth. Alternatively, transfer the soup to a blender and blend in batches.

4. Return the soup to the pot and heat through.

5. Serve warm and enjoy the comforting flavors.

Recipe 18: Vegan Ratatouille

Ingredients:

- 1 organic eggplant, cubed
- 2 organic zucchinis, sliced
- 1 organic red bell pepper, diced
- 1 organic yellow bell pepper, diced
- 1 organic onion, chopped
- 3 cloves organic garlic, minced
- 1 can (15 oz) organic diced tomatoes
- 2 tbsp organic tomato paste
- 2 tbsp organic olive oil
- 1 tsp organic dried thyme
- 1 tsp organic dried rosemary
- 1/2 tsp organic dried basil
- Salt and pepper to taste
- Fresh organic basil leaves for garnish

Instructions:

1. Preheat your oven to 375°F (190°C).

2. In a large ovenproof skillet, heat olive oil over medium heat.

3. Sauté onion and garlic until fragrant.

4. Add eggplant, zucchinis, red and yellow bell peppers, diced tomatoes, tomato paste, thyme, rosemary, basil, salt, and pepper. Stir to combine.

5. Cover and transfer the skillet to the oven. Bake for 25-30 minutes or until the vegetables are tender.

6. Garnish with fresh basil leaves before serving.

Recipe 19: Vegan Tofu and Vegetable Stir-Fry

Ingredients:

- 2 cups organic broccoli florets
- 1 cup organic bell peppers, sliced
- 1 cup organic snap peas
- 1 cup organic carrots, sliced
- 1 cup organic mushrooms, sliced
- 1 cup organic extra-firm tofu, cubed
- 3 tbsp organic low-sodium soy sauce or tamari
- 2 tbsp organic hoisin sauce
- 1 tbsp organic sesame oil
- 2 cloves organic garlic, minced
- 1 tsp organic ginger, minced
- Cooked organic brown rice or quinoa for serving

Instructions:

1. In a large skillet or wok, heat sesame oil over medium-high heat.

2. Add broccoli, bell peppers, snap peas, carrots, mushrooms, and tofu. Stir-fry until the vegetables are tender and tofu is slightly crispy.

3. In a small bowl, whisk together garlic, soy sauce or tamari, hoisin sauce, and ginger.

4. Add the sauce to the stir-fry and toss to coat the vegetables and tofu.

5. Serve over cooked brown rice or quinoa.

Recipe 20: Vegan Mushroom Risotto

Ingredients:

- 2 cups organic Arborio rice
- 1 cup organic white mushrooms, sliced
- 1 cup organic shiitake mushrooms, sliced
- 1 cup organic cremini mushrooms, sliced
- 1 organic onion, chopped
- 2 cloves organic garlic, minced
- 1/2 cup organic white wine

- 4 cups organic vegetable broth
- 1/4 cup organic nutritional yeast (optional)
- 2 tbsp organic olive oil
- Salt and pepper to taste
- Fresh organic parsley for garnish
Instructions:
1. In a large pot, bring vegetable broth to a simmer and keep it warm.
2. In a separate large pot, heat olive oil over medium heat.
3. Sauté onion and garlic until fragrant.
4. Add the Arborio rice and cook for a few minutes until it becomes translucent.
5. Pour in white wine and stir until it's mostly absorbed.
6. Begin adding vegetable broth one ladle at a time, stirring until the liquid is mostly absorbed before adding more.
7. Continue this process until the rice is creamy and tender (about 18-20 minutes).
8. In a skillet, sauté the sliced mushrooms until they release their liquid and become tender.
9. Stir the cooked mushrooms into the risotto.
10. Season with salt and pepper, and add nutritional yeast if desired.
11. Garnish with fresh parsley before serving.

These 20 organic vegan recipes offer a diverse selection of delicious dishes to continue your 90-day Ultimate Lifestyle Transformation. As you explore these recipes, you'll experience the joy of flavorful, nutritious meals that support your plant-based journey and help you thrive on a daily basis. Enjoy the culinary adventure!

Recipe 21: Vegan Sweet Potato and Kale Hash
Ingredients:
- 2 organic sweet potatoes, peeled and diced
- 1 organic onion, chopped
- 2 cups organic kale, chopped
- 2 cloves organic garlic, minced

- 2 tbsp organic olive oil
- 1 tsp organic smoked paprika
- Salt and pepper to taste
Instructions:
1. In a large skillet, heat olive oil over medium heat.
2. Sauté onion and garlic until fragrant.
3. Add sweet potatoes and cook until they're tender and slightly crispy.
4. Stir in kale and cook until wilted.
5. Season with smoked paprika, salt, and pepper.
6. Serve as a hearty and healthy breakfast or brunch option.
Recipe 22: Vegan Turmeric and Ginger Detox Tea
Ingredients:
- 1 cup organic hot water
- 1 organic turmeric tea bag (or 1 tsp organic ground turmeric)
- 1 tsp organic ginger, grated
- 1 tsp organic lemon juice
- 1 tsp organic maple syrup (optional for sweetness)
Instructions:
1. Steep the turmeric tea bag or ground turmeric in hot water for 5-7 minutes.
2. Remove the tea bag or strain the tea if using ground turmeric.
3. Stir in grated ginger, lemon juice, and maple syrup (if desired).
4. Enjoy this soothing and detoxifying tea.
Recipe 23: Vegan Spinach and Pineapple Smoothie Bowl
Ingredients:
- 2 cups organic spinach
- 1 cup frozen organic pineapple chunks
- 1 organic banana
- 1 cup organic almond milk
- 1 tbsp organic chia seeds
- 1 tsp organic spirulina powder

- 1 tbsp Coco-Hydrate[3] (Use gift Code EMPATHY for discount)

Instructions:

1. Blend spinach, frozen pineapple, banana, and almond milk until smooth.

2. Pour the smoothie into a bowl.

3. Top with chia seeds and, if desired, a sprinkle of spirulina powder for added nutrition.

Recipe 24: Vegan Acai Berry Bowl

Ingredients:

- 2 organic frozen acai berry packets

- 1 organic banana

- 1/2 cup organic blueberries

- 1/2 cup organic strawberries

- 1/4 cup organic granola

- 1 tbsp organic almond butter

- 1 tbsp organic Bio Fruit[4] (Use gift Code EMPATHY for discount)

Instructions:

1. Blend the frozen acai berry packets, banana, blueberries, and strawberries until smooth.

2. Pour the acai mixture into a bowl.

3. Top with granola, almond butter, and, if desired, a sprinkle of maca powder for extra energy.

Recipe 25: Vegan Green Superfood Smoothie Bowl

Ingredients:

- 2 cups organic spinach

- 1 organic banana

- 1/2 organic avocado

- 1 cup organic almond milk

- 1 tbsp organic chia seeds

---

3.   https://ishoppurium.com/AllProducts/2754

4.   https://ishoppurium.com/AllProducts/2491

- 1 tbsp organic ancient Kamut[5] wheatgrass powder (Use gift Code EMPATHY for discount)

Instructions:

1. Blend spinach, banana, avocado, and almond milk until smooth.

2. Pour the green smoothie into a bowl.

3. Top with chia seeds and, if desired, a sprinkle of wheatgrass powder for added nutrients.

Recipe 26: Vegan Chia Seed Pudding with Berries

Ingredients:

- 3 tbsp organic chia seeds

- 1 cup organic almond milk

- 1/2 tsp organic vanilla extract

- 1 tsp organic maple syrup

- 1/2 cup organic mixed berries (e.g., strawberries, blueberries, raspberries)

- 1 tbsp organic hemp seeds (optional, for a superfood boost)

Instructions:

1. In a jar, combine chia seeds, almond milk, vanilla extract, and maple syrup. Stir well.

2. Refrigerate the mixture for at least 2 hours or overnight to thicken.

3. Top the chia pudding with mixed berries and, if desired, a sprinkle of hemp seeds for added protein.

Recipe 27: Vegan Detox Green Smoothie

Ingredients:

- 2 cups organic spinach

- 1 organic apple, cored and chopped

- 1/2 organic cucumber, sliced

- 1 organic lemon, juiced

- 1 tbsp organic fresh ginger, grated

- 1 cup organic coconut water

- 1 tsp organic spirulina powder

---

5.   https://ishoppurium.com/AllProducts/2422

Instructions:

1. Blend spinach, apple, cucumber, lemon juice, ginger, and coconut water until smooth.

2. Add spirulina powder (if desired) and blend again.

3. Serve this detoxifying green smoothie to kickstart your day.

Recipe 28: Vegan Blueberry Bliss Smoothie Bowl

Ingredients:

- 1 cup organic blueberries

- 1 organic banana

- 1 cup organic almond milk

- 1/2 cup organic oats

- 1 tbsp organic chia seeds

- 1 tsp organic acai powder

Instructions:

1. Blend blueberries, banana, almond milk, and oats until smooth.

2. Pour the smoothie into a bowl.

3. Top with chia seeds and, if desired, a sprinkle of acai powder for antioxidant power.

Recipe 29: Vegan Spicy Quinoa and Black Bean Salad

Ingredients:

- 1 cup organic quinoa

- 1 can (15 oz) organic black beans, drained and rinsed

- 1 cup organic corn kernels (fresh or frozen)

- 1/2 cup organic red bell pepper, diced

- 1/2 cup organic red onion, finely chopped

- 1/4 cup organic cilantro, chopped

- 2 tbsp organic lime juice

- 2 tbsp organic olive oil

- 1 tsp organic chili powder

- 1/2 tsp organic cayenne pepper (adjust to your spice preference)

- Salt and pepper to taste

Instructions:

1. Cook quinoa according to package instructions and let it cool.

2. In a large bowl, combine quinoa, black beans, corn, red bell pepper, red onion, and cilantro.

3. In a small bowl, whisk together lime juice, olive oil, chili powder, cayenne pepper, salt, and pepper.

4. Pour the dressing over the salad and toss to combine.

5. Serve this spicy salad with a kick of heat.

Recipe 30: Vegan Matcha Green Tea Smoothie Bowl

Ingredients:

- 2 tsp organic matcha green tea powder[6](Use gift Code EMPATHY for discount)

- 1 organic banana

- 1/2 cup organic almond milk

- 1/2 cup organic Vegan Greek yogurt

- 1 tbsp organic maple syrup

- 1/4 cup organic granola

- Sliced organic kiwi and strawberries for topping

Instructions:

1. In a blender, combine matcha powder, banana, almond milk, Greek yogurt, or maple syrup. Blend until smooth.

2. Pour

the matcha mixture into a bowl.

3. Top with granola, sliced kiwi, and strawberries for a refreshing and energizing breakfast.

Recipe 31: Vegan Peanut Butter and Chocolate Smoothie Bowl

Ingredients:

- 2 tbsp organic peanut butter

- 1 organic banana

- 1 cup organic almond milk

- 1 tbsp organic cocoa powder

- 1 tbsp organic chia seeds

---

6.   https://ishoppurium.com/AllProducts/2782

- 1 tsp organic maca powder
- Sliced organic bananas and chopped organic peanuts for topping
Instructions:
1. Blend peanut butter, banana, almond milk, cocoa powder, chia seeds, and maca powder (if using) until smooth.

2. Pour the peanut butter-chocolate smoothie into a bowl.

3. Top with sliced bananas and chopped peanuts for a delightful treat.

Recipe 32: Vegan Roasted Beet and Quinoa Salad
Ingredients:
- 2 organic beets, peeled and diced
- 1 cup organic quinoa
- 2 cups organic vegetable broth
- 1/4 cup organic walnuts, chopped
- 1/4 cup organic dried cranberries
- 2 tbsp organic balsamic vinegar
- 2 tbsp organic olive oil
- 1 tsp organic Dijon mustard
- Salt and pepper to taste
Instructions:
1. Preheat your oven to 400°F (200°C).

2. Toss diced beets with a bit of olive oil, salt, and pepper. Roast for 30-35 minutes until tender.

3. In a pot, bring vegetable broth to a boil and add quinoa. Cook until fluffy and the broth is absorbed.

4. In a large bowl, combine cooked quinoa, roasted beets, walnuts, and dried cranberries.

5. In a small bowl, whisk together balsamic vinegar, olive oil, Dijon mustard, salt, and pepper. Drizzle over the salad and toss to combine.

6. Enjoy this vibrant and nutrient-packed salad.

Recipe 33: Vegan Mango and Turmeric Smoothie Bowl
Ingredients:

- 1 organic mango, peeled and diced
- 1 organic banana
- 1 cup organic coconut milk
- 1 tsp organic turmeric powder
- 1 tbsp organic flaxseeds
- 1 tsp organic maple syrup (optional for sweetness)
- Sliced organic kiwi and coconut flakes for topping
Instructions:
1. Blend mango, banana, coconut milk, turmeric powder, flaxseeds, and honey or maple syrup (if using) until smooth.
2. Pour the mango-turmeric smoothie into a bowl.
3. Top with sliced kiwi and coconut flakes for a tropical delight.
Recipe 34: Vegan Superfood Smoothie Bowl
Ingredients:
- 2 cups organic spinach
- 1 organic banana
- 1/2 cup organic blueberries
- 1/2 cup organic raspberries
- 1 cup organic almond milk
- 1 tbsp organic chia seeds
- 1 tsp organic acai powder
Instructions:
1. Blend spinach, banana, blueberries, raspberries, and almond milk until smooth.
2. Pour the superfood smoothie into a bowl.
3. Top with chia seeds and, if desired, a sprinkle of acai powder for added antioxidants.
Recipe 35: Vegan Cauliflower and Chickpea Curry
Ingredients:
- 1 small organic cauliflower, cut into florets
- 1 can (15 oz) organic chickpeas, drained and rinsed
- 1 organic onion, chopped

- 2 cloves organic garlic, minced
- 1 can (15 oz) organic diced tomatoes
- 1 can (15 oz) organic coconut milk
- 2 tbsp organic curry powder
- 1 tsp organic ground cumin
- 1/2 tsp organic turmeric
- 1/2 tsp organic paprika
- Salt and pepper to taste
- Fresh organic cilantro for garnish
- Cooked organic brown rice or quinoa for serving
Instructions:
1. In a large skillet, sauté onion and garlic until fragrant.
2. Stir in cauliflower florets and cook for a few minutes.
3. Add chickpeas, diced tomatoes, coconut milk, curry powder, cumin, turmeric, paprika, salt, and pepper. Stir well.
4. Cover and simmer for 20-25 minutes or until the cauliflower is tender.
5. Serve the cauliflower and chickpea curry over cooked brown rice or quinoa. Garnish with fresh cilantro.
Recipe 36: Vegan Almond and Raspberry Chia Pudding
Ingredients:
- 3 tbsp organic chia seeds
- 1 cup organic almond milk
- 1/2 tsp organic almond extract
- 1/2 cup organic raspberries
- 1 tbsp organic sliced almonds
- 1 tsp organic maple syrup (optional for sweetness)
Instructions:
1. In a jar, combine chia seeds, almond milk, almond extract or maple syrup (if using). Stir well.
2. Refrigerate the mixture for at least 2 hours or overnight to thicken.

3. Top the almond and raspberry chia pudding with raspberries and sliced almonds. Enjoy this creamy and nutritious treat.

Recipe 37: Vegan Citrus and Beet Smoothie Bowl

Ingredients:

- 1 organic beet, peeled and diced
- 1 organic orange, peeled and segmented
- 1 organic banana
- 1 cup organic almond milk
- 1 tbsp organic hemp seeds
- 1 tsp organic ginger, grated
- 1 tsp organic honey or maple syrup (optional for sweetness)
- Sliced organic kiwi and orange zest for topping

Instructions:

1. Blend beet, orange segments, banana, almond milk, hemp seeds, ginger, and honey or maple syrup (if using) until smooth.

2. Pour the citrus and beet smoothie into a bowl.

3. Top with sliced kiwi and a sprinkle of orange zest for a refreshing start to your day.

Recipe 38: Vegan Broccoli and Kale Detox Salad

Ingredients:

- 2 cups organic broccoli florets
- 2 cups organic kale, chopped
- 1/4 cup organic red onion, finely chopped
- 1/4 cup organic raisins
- 1/4 cup organic sunflower seeds
- 2 tbsp organic apple cider vinegar
- 2 tbsp organic olive oil
- 1 tsp organic Dijon mustard
- 1 tsp organic maple syrup
- Salt and pepper to taste

Instructions:

1. Steam broccoli florets until they're tender-crisp and let them cool.

2. In a large bowl, combine steamed broccoli, kale, red onion, raisins, and sunflower seeds.

3. In a small bowl, whisk together apple cider vinegar, olive oil, Dijon mustard, maple syrup, salt, and pepper.

4. Pour the dressing over the salad and toss to combine.

5. Enjoy this detoxifying and crunchy salad.

Recipe 39: Vegan Spirulina and Berry Smoothie Bowl

Ingredients:

- 1 frozen organic banana

- 1 cup frozen organic mixed berries (blueberries, blackberries, raspberries)

- 1 tsp organic spirulina powder

- 1 cup organic spinach or kale

- 1/2 cup organic almond milk

- Toppings: Sliced organic banana, fresh organic berries, chia seeds, shredded coconut, and granola

Instructions:

1. In a high-speed blender, combine the frozen banana, frozen mixed berries, spirulina powder, spinach or kale, and almond milk.

2. Blend until the mixture is smooth and creamy.

3. Pour the smoothie into a bowl.

4. Top with sliced banana, fresh berries, chia seeds, shredded coconut, and granola for added texture and flavor.

5. Enjoy your vibrant and nutrient-packed spirulina and berry smoothie bowl!

Recipe 40: Vegan Teriyaki Tofu Stir-Fry

Ingredients:

- 1 cup organic brown rice

- 1 cup organic extra-firm tofu, cubed

- 2 cups organic broccoli florets

- 1 cup organic snap peas

- 1 cup organic carrots, sliced

- 1/4 cup organic low-sodium soy sauce or tamari
- 2 tbsp organic teriyaki sauce
- 1 tbsp organic sesame oil
- 1 tbsp organic rice vinegar
- 2 cloves organic garlic, minced
- 1 tsp organic ginger, minced
- Sesame seeds and chopped green onions for garnish
Instructions:
1. Cook brown rice according to package instructions and set aside.
2. In a large skillet, heat sesame oil over medium-high heat.
3. Add tofu and sauté until it's lightly browned on all sides. Remove tofu from the skillet and set aside.
4. In the same skillet, add garlic and ginger, and sauté until fragrant.
5. Add broccoli, snap peas, and carrots, and stir-fry until the vegetables are tender-crisp.
6. In a small bowl, whisk together soy sauce or tamari, teriyaki sauce, and rice vinegar.
7. Return the tofu to the skillet, and pour the sauce over the tofu and vegetables. Stir to coat and heat through.
8. Serve the teriyaki tofu stir-fry over cooked brown rice, and garnish with sesame seeds and chopped green onions.

Certainly! Here are 10 meal prep-friendly organic vegan recipes that can be made in batches to last for at least 5 days:

Recipe 41: Vegan Chickpea and Vegetable Curry
Ingredients:
- 2 tbsp organic coconut oil
- 1 organic onion, chopped
- 3 cloves organic garlic, minced
- 1 organic bell pepper, diced
- 2 cups organic cauliflower florets
- 2 cups organic carrots, sliced
- 4 cups organic chickpeas, cooked

- 1 can (28 oz) organic diced tomatoes
- 2 cans (28 oz) organic coconut milk
- 3 tbsp organic curry powder
- 2 tsp organic cumin
- 2 tsp organic ground coriander
- Salt and pepper to taste

Instructions:

1. In a large pot, heat coconut oil over medium heat.
2. Add onion and garlic, and sauté until fragrant.
3. Stir in bell pepper, cauliflower, and carrots, and cook for a few minutes.
4. Add curry powder, cumin, and coriander. Cook for another minute.
5. Add chickpeas, diced tomatoes, and coconut milk.
6. Bring to a boil, reduce heat, and simmer for 20-25 minutes.
7. Season with salt and pepper.
8. Divide into airtight containers for meal prep.

Recipe 42: Vegan Lentil and Sweet Potato Stew

Ingredients:

- 2 tbsp organic olive oil
- 2 organic onions, chopped
- 4 cloves organic garlic, minced
- 2 organic sweet potatoes, peeled and diced
- 2 cups organic brown or green lentils
- 8 cups organic vegetable broth
- 2 cans (28 oz) organic diced tomatoes
- 4 tsp organic ground cumin
- 2 tsp organic ground coriander
- 2 tsp organic smoked paprika
- Salt and pepper to taste
- 8 cups organic kale, chopped

Instructions:

1. In a large pot, heat olive oil over medium heat.

2. Add onions and garlic, and sauté until fragrant.

3. Stir in sweet potatoes, lentils, vegetable broth, diced tomatoes, cumin, coriander, smoked paprika, salt, and pepper.

4. Bring to a boil, then reduce heat and simmer for 25-30 minutes.

5. Stir in chopped kale and cook for a few more minutes until wilted.

6. Portion into containers for meal prep.

Recipe 43: Vegan Quinoa and Black Bean Salad

Ingredients:

- 2 cups organic quinoa

- 4 cups organic vegetable broth

- 2 cans (28 oz) organic black beans, drained and rinsed

- 2 cups organic cherry tomatoes, halved

- 1 cup organic red onion, finely chopped

- 1/2 cup organic cilantro, chopped

- 4 tbsp organic lime juice

- 4 tbsp organic olive oil

- Salt and pepper to taste

Instructions:

1. In a large pot, bring vegetable broth to a boil and add quinoa. Cook until the broth is absorbed.

2. In a large bowl, combine cooked quinoa, black beans, cherry tomatoes, red onion, and cilantro.

3. In a small bowl, whisk together lime juice, olive oil, salt, and pepper.

4. Pour the dressing over the salad and toss to combine.

5. Divide into containers for meal prep.

Recipe 44: Vegan Teriyaki Tofu Stir-Fry

Ingredients:

- 2 cups organic brown rice

- 2 cups organic extra-firm tofu, cubed

- 4 cups organic broccoli florets

- 2 cups organic snap peas
- 2 cups organic carrots, sliced
- 1/2 cup organic low-sodium soy sauce or tamari
- 4 tbsp organic teriyaki sauce
- 2 tbsp organic sesame oil
- 2 tbsp organic rice vinegar
- 4 cloves organic garlic, minced
- 2 tsp organic ginger, minced
- Sesame seeds and chopped green onions for garnish
Instructions:
1. Cook brown rice according to package instructions.
2. In a large skillet or wok, heat sesame oil over medium-high heat.
3. Add tofu and sauté until it's lightly browned on all sides. Remove tofu from the skillet and set aside.
4. In the same skillet, add garlic and ginger, and sauté until fragrant.
5. Add broccoli, snap peas, and carrots, and stir-fry until the vegetables are tender-crisp.
6. In a small bowl, whisk together soy sauce or tamari, teriyaki sauce, and rice vinegar.
7. Return the tofu to the skillet, and pour the sauce over the tofu and vegetables. Stir to coat and heat through.
8. Portion into containers for meal prep.
Recipe 45: Vegan Mediterranean Quinoa Salad
Ingredients:
- 2 cups organic quinoa
- 4 cups organic vegetable broth
- 2 cans (28 oz) organic chickpeas, drained and rinsed
- 2 cups organic cucumber, diced
- 2 cups organic cherry tomatoes, halved
- 1 cup organic red onion, finely chopped
- 1 cup organic Kalamata olives, pitted and sliced
- 1 cup organic fresh parsley, chopped

- 8 tbsp organic extra-virgin olive oil

- 4 tbsp organic lemon juice

- 4 tsp organic dried oregano

- Salt and pepper to taste

Instructions:

1. In a large pot, bring vegetable broth to a boil and add quinoa. Cook until the broth is absorbed.

2. In a large bowl, combine cooked quinoa, chickpeas, cucumber, cherry tomatoes, red onion, olives, and parsley.

3. In a small bowl, whisk together olive oil, lemon juice, dried oregano, salt, and pepper.

4. Pour the dressing over the salad and toss to combine.

5. Divide into containers for meal prep.

Recipe 46: Vegan Ratatouille

Ingredients:

- 4 organic eggplants, cubed

- 8 organic zucchinis, sliced

- 4 organic red bell peppers, diced

- 4 organic yellow bell peppers, diced

- 4 organic onions, chopped

- 12 cloves organic garlic, minced

- 4 cans (28 oz) organic diced tomatoes

- 8 tbsp organic tomato paste

- 8 tbsp organic olive oil

- 4 tsp organic dried thyme

- 4 tsp organic dried rosemary

- 2 tsp organic dried basil

- Salt and pepper to taste

- Fresh organic basil leaves for garnish

Instructions:

1. In a large ovenproof skillet, heat olive oil over medium heat.

2. Sauté onions and garlic until fragrant.

3. Add eggplants, zucchinis, red and yellow bell peppers, diced tomatoes, tomato paste, thyme, rosemary, basil, salt, and pepper. Stir to combine.

4. Cover and transfer the skillet to the oven. Bake for 25-30 minutes.

5. Garnish with fresh basil leaves before dividing into containers for meal prep.

**Recipe 47:

Vegan Tofu and Vegetable Stir-Fry**

Ingredients:

- 4 cups organic brown rice

- 4 cups organic extra-firm tofu, cubed

- 8 cups organic broccoli florets

- 4 cups organic snap peas

- 4 cups organic carrots, sliced

- 1 cup organic mushrooms, sliced

- 1 cup organic bell peppers, sliced

- 1 cup organic snap peas

- 1 cup organic snow peas

- 1 cup organic baby corn

- 1/2 cup organic low-sodium soy sauce or tamari

- 1/4 cup organic hoisin sauce

- 2 tbsp organic sesame oil

- 8 cloves organic garlic, minced

- 4 tsp organic ginger, minced

Instructions:

1. Cook brown rice according to package instructions.

2. In a large skillet or wok, heat sesame oil over medium-high heat.

3. Add tofu and sauté until it's lightly browned on all sides. Remove tofu from the skillet and set aside.

4. In the same skillet, add garlic and ginger, and sauté until fragrant.

5. Stir in broccoli, snap peas, carrots, mushrooms, bell peppers, snap peas, snow peas, and baby corn. Stir-fry until the vegetables are tender-crisp.

6. In a small bowl, whisk together soy sauce or tamari and hoisin sauce.

7. Return the tofu to the skillet, and pour the sauce over the tofu and vegetables. Stir to coat and heat through.

8. Portion into containers for meal prep.

Recipe 48: Vegan Spinach and Mushroom Stuffed Portobello Mushrooms

Ingredients:

- 10 large organic portobello mushrooms
- 5 tbsp organic olive oil
- 5 organic onions, chopped
- 10 cloves organic garlic, minced
- 10 cups organic baby spinach
- 5 cups organic mushrooms, finely chopped
- 2.5 cups organic vegan cream cheese
- 1.25 cups organic breadcrumbs
- 1.25 cups organic vegan Parmesan cheese (optional)
- Salt and pepper to taste

Instructions:

1. Preheat your oven to 375°F (190°C).

2. Remove the stems from the portobello mushrooms and set aside.

3. In a large skillet, heat olive oil over medium heat.

4. Sauté onions and garlic until fragrant.

5. Add baby spinach and mushrooms, and cook until they are wilted and tender.

6. In a bowl, combine the sautéed mixture with vegan cream cheese, breadcrumbs, and vegan Parmesan cheese (if using). Season with salt and pepper.

7. Stuff the portobello mushrooms with the mixture.

8. Place the stuffed mushrooms in a baking dish and bake for 20-25 minutes.

9. Divide into containers for meal prep.

Recipe 49: Vegan Lentil and Vegetable Curry

Ingredients:

- 3 cups organic brown lentils
- 6 cups organic vegetable broth
- 3 tbsp organic coconut oil
- 3 organic onions, chopped
- 9 cloves organic garlic, minced
- 3 organic bell peppers, diced
- 6 cups organic cauliflower florets
- 6 cups organic carrots, sliced
- 3 cans (42 oz) organic diced tomatoes
- 9 tbsp organic curry powder
- 6 tsp organic cumin
- 6 tsp organic ground coriander
- Salt and pepper to taste

Instructions:

1. In a large pot, heat coconut oil over medium heat.

2. Add onions and garlic, and sauté until fragrant.

3. Stir in bell peppers, cauliflower, and carrots, and cook for a few minutes.

4. Add curry powder, cumin, and coriander. Cook for another minute.

5. Add lentils, vegetable broth, diced tomatoes, salt, and pepper.

6. Bring to a boil, reduce heat, and simmer for 25-30 minutes.

7. Divide into containers for meal prep.

Recipe 50: Vegan Quinoa and Vegetable Stir-Fry

Ingredients:

- 4 cups organic quinoa
- 4 cups organic extra-firm tofu, cubed

- 8 cups organic broccoli florets
- 4 cups organic snap peas
- 4 cups organic carrots, sliced
- 2 cups organic bell peppers, sliced
- 2 cups organic mushrooms, sliced
- 1 cup organic snow peas
- 1 cup organic baby corn
- 1/2 cup organic low-sodium soy sauce or tamari
- 1/4 cup organic hoisin sauce
- 2 tbsp organic sesame oil
- 4 cloves organic garlic, minced
- 2 tsp organic ginger, minced

Instructions:

1. Cook quinoa according to package instructions.

2. In a large skillet or wok, heat sesame oil over medium-high heat.

3. Add tofu and sauté until it's lightly browned on all sides. Remove tofu from the skillet and set aside.

4. In the same skillet, add garlic and ginger, and sauté until fragrant.

5. Stir in broccoli, snap peas, carrots, bell peppers, mushrooms, snow peas, and baby corn. Stir-fry until the vegetables are tender-crisp.

6. In a small bowl, whisk together soy sauce or tamari and hoisin sauce.

7. Return the tofu to the skillet, and pour the sauce over the tofu and vegetables. Stir to coat and heat through.

8. Divide into containers for meal prep.

These 10 meal prep-friendly organic vegan recipes will help you maintain a consistent and nutritious plant-based meal plan for at least 5 days. Enjoy the convenience of having delicious and healthy meals ready to go!

Certainly! Here are 10 high-protein organic vegan recipes to help you meet your protein needs:

Recipe 51: Vegan Chickpea and Spinach Curry

Ingredients:
- 2 cups organic quinoa
- 4 cups organic vegetable broth
- 2 cans (28 oz) organic chickpeas, drained and rinsed
- 4 cups organic spinach
- 2 cups organic diced tomatoes
- 2 cups organic coconut milk
- 4 tbsp organic curry powder
- 2 tsp organic cumin
- 2 tsp organic coriander
- Salt and pepper to taste

Instructions:

1. In a large pot, bring vegetable broth to a boil and add quinoa. Cook until the broth is absorbed.

2. In a separate pot, combine chickpeas, spinach, diced tomatoes, coconut milk, curry powder, cumin, coriander, salt, and pepper.

3. Bring to a simmer and cook for 15-20 minutes.

4. Serve the chickpea and spinach curry over cooked quinoa.

Recipe 52: Vegan Tofu and Black Bean Tacos

Ingredients:
- 1 block (14 oz) organic extra-firm tofu, crumbled
- 1 can (15 oz) organic black beans, drained and rinsed
- 1 organic bell pepper, diced
- 1 organic onion, chopped
- 2 cloves organic garlic, minced
- 2 tsp organic chili powder
- 1 tsp organic cumin
- 1/2 tsp organic paprika
- 1/2 tsp organic cayenne pepper (adjust to your spice preference)
- Salt and pepper to taste
- 8 organic whole-wheat or corn tortillas

- Toppings: Sliced avocado, salsa, shredded lettuce, and vegan sour cream

Instructions:

1. In a skillet, sauté crumbled tofu, black beans, bell pepper, onion, and garlic until the tofu is slightly browned.

2. Stir in chili powder, cumin, paprika, cayenne pepper, salt, and pepper.

3. Warm the tortillas and fill with the tofu and black bean mixture.

4. Top with sliced avocado, salsa, shredded lettuce, and vegan sour cream.

Recipe 53: Vegan Lentil and Vegetable Stir-Fry

Ingredients:

- 2 cups organic brown lentils
- 4 cups organic vegetable broth
- 1/4 cup organic low-sodium soy sauce or tamari
- 2 tbsp organic sesame oil
- 4 cloves organic garlic, minced
- 2 tsp organic ginger, minced
- 4 cups organic broccoli florets
- 2 cups organic bell peppers, sliced
- 2 cups organic snap peas
- 2 cups organic carrots, sliced
- 1 cup organic mushrooms, sliced
- 1 cup organic snow peas
- 1 cup organic baby corn
- 1/4 cup chopped organic green onions

Instructions:

1. In a large pot, bring vegetable broth to a boil and add lentils. Cook until lentils are tender and the broth is absorbed.

2. In a large skillet or wok, heat sesame oil over medium-high heat.

3. Add garlic and ginger, and sauté until fragrant.

4. Stir in broccoli, bell peppers, snap peas, carrots, mushrooms, snow peas, and baby corn. Stir-fry until the vegetables are tender-crisp.

5. Add cooked lentils and soy sauce or tamari. Stir to combine and heat through.

6. Garnish with chopped green onions.

Recipe 54: Vegan Seitan and Vegetable Stir-Fry

Ingredients:

- 2 cups organic brown rice
- 2 cups organic seitan, sliced
- 4 cups organic broccoli florets
- 2 cups organic bell peppers, sliced
- 2 cups organic snap peas
- 2 cups organic carrots, sliced
- 1 cup organic mushrooms, sliced
- 1/4 cup organic low-sodium soy sauce or tamari
- 2 tbsp organic sesame oil
- 4 cloves organic garlic, minced
- 2 tsp organic ginger, minced
- Sesame seeds and chopped green onions for garnish

Instructions:

1. Cook brown rice according to package instructions.

2. In a large skillet or wok, heat sesame oil over medium-high heat.

3. Add seitan and sauté until it's slightly browned.

4. Add garlic and ginger, and sauté until fragrant.

5. Stir in broccoli, bell peppers, snap peas, carrots, mushrooms, and seitan. Stir-fry until the vegetables are tender-crisp.

6. In a small bowl, whisk together soy sauce or tamari.

7. Pour the sauce over the stir-fry and toss to coat.

8. Serve over cooked brown rice and garnish with sesame seeds and chopped green onions.

Recipe 55: Vegan Tempeh and Kale Salad

Ingredients:

- 1 package (8 oz) organic tempeh, cubed
- 4 cups organic kale, chopped
- 2 cups organic cherry tomatoes, halved
- 1/2 cup organic red onion, finely chopped
- 1/4 cup organic sunflower seeds
- 1/4 cup organic balsamic vinaigrette dressing
- Salt and pepper to taste

Instructions:

1. Steam the tempeh cubes for 10-15 minutes to soften and prepare them for absorption of flavors.

2. In a large bowl, combine chopped kale, cherry tomatoes, red onion, and steamed tempeh.

3. Drizzle with balsamic vinaigrette dressing and toss to combine.

4. Season with salt and pepper.

5. Sprinkle with sunflower seeds for added crunch.

Recipe 56: Vegan Red Lentil and Spinach Soup

Ingredients:

- 1 cup organic red lentils
- 4 cups organic vegetable broth
- 1 organic onion, chopped
- 2 cloves organic garlic, minced
- 1 tsp organic cumin
- 1/2 tsp organic paprika
- 1/2 tsp organic ground coriander
- 4 cups organic spinach
- Juice of 1 organic lemon
- Salt and pepper to taste

Instructions:

1. In a large pot, combine red lentils, vegetable broth, onion, garlic, cumin, paprika, and coriander.

2. Bring to a boil, then reduce heat and simmer for 20-25 minutes or until the lentils are tender.

3. Stir in spinach and cook until wilted.

4. Add lemon juice and season with salt and pepper.

Recipe 57: Vegan Quinoa and Black Bean Salad

Ingredients:

- 2 cups organic quinoa

- 4 cups organic vegetable broth

- 2 cans (28 oz) organic black beans, drained and rinsed

- 2 cups organic cherry tomatoes, halved

- 1 cup organic red onion, finely chopped

- 1/2 cup organic cilantro, chopped

- 4 tbsp organic lime juice

- 4 tbsp organic olive oil

- Salt and pepper to taste

Instructions:

1. In a large pot, bring vegetable broth to a boil and add quinoa. Cook until the broth is absorbed.

2. In a large bowl, combine cooked quinoa, black beans, cherry tomatoes, red onion, and cilantro.

3. In a small bowl, whisk together lime juice, olive oil, salt, and pepper.

4. Pour the dressing over the salad and toss to combine.

Recipe 58: Vegan Lentil and Mushroom Stroganoff

Ingredients:

- 2 cups organic brown rice or whole-wheat pasta

- 2 cups organic brown lentils

- 4 cups organic vegetable broth

- 2 cups organic mushrooms, sliced

- 1 cup organic onion, chopped

- 2 cloves organic garlic, minced

- 2 tbsp organic olive oil

- 1 cup organic coconut milk

- 2 tbsp organic nutritional yeast

- 1 tsp organic thyme
- Salt and pepper to taste
- Chopped fresh parsley for garnish

Instructions:

1. Cook brown rice or whole-wheat pasta according to package instructions.

2. In a large pot, bring vegetable broth to a boil and add lentils. Cook until the broth is absorbed.

3. In a skillet, heat olive oil over medium heat.

4. Sauté onions and garlic until fragrant.

5. Add mushrooms and cook until they release their liquid and become tender.

6. Stir in cooked lentils, coconut milk, nutritional yeast, thyme, salt, and pepper.

7. Simmer for a few minutes until the sauce thickens.

8. Serve the lentil and mushroom stroganoff over cooked brown rice or pasta, and garnish with chopped fresh parsley.

Recipe 59: Vegan Black Bean and Quinoa Stuffed Peppers

Ingredients:

- 4 large organic bell peppers
- 1 cup organic quinoa
- 2 cups organic vegetable broth
- 2 cans (28 oz) organic black beans, drained and rinsed
- 1 cup organic corn kernels
- 1 cup organic diced tomatoes
- 1 cup organic red onion, finely chopped
- 1 tsp organic chili powder
- 1/2 tsp organic cumin
- Salt and pepper to taste
- 1 cup organic tomato sauce
- 1 cup organic vegan cheese shreds (optional)
- Fresh organic cilantro for garnish

Instructions:

1. Preheat your oven to 375°F (190°C).

2. Cut the tops off the bell peppers, remove the seeds, and set aside.

3. In a large pot, bring vegetable broth to a boil and add quinoa. Cook until the broth is absorbed.

4. In a large bowl, combine cooked quinoa, black beans, corn, diced tomatoes, red onion, chili powder, cumin, salt, and pepper.

5. Stuff the bell peppers with the quinoa and black bean mixture.

6. Place the stuffed peppers in a baking dish, and pour tomato sauce over them.

7. Cover with foil and bake for 25-30 minutes.

8. If desired, sprinkle vegan cheese shreds on top and bake for an additional 5 minutes or until they melt.

9. Garnish with fresh cilantro before serving.

Recipe 60: Vegan Tempeh and Broccoli Stir-Fry

Ingredients:

- 2 cups organic brown rice

- 2 cups organic tempeh, cubed

- 4 cups organic broccoli florets

- 2 cups organic bell peppers, sliced

- 2 cups organic snap peas

- 2 cups organic carrots, sliced

- 1/4 cup organic low-sodium soy sauce or tamari

- 2 tbsp organic sesame oil

- 4 cloves organic garlic, minced

- 2 tsp organic ginger, minced

- Sesame seeds and chopped green onions for garnish

Instructions:

1. Cook brown rice according to package instructions.

2. In a large skillet or wok, heat sesame oil over medium-high heat.

3. Add tempeh and sauté until it's slightly browned.

4. Add garlic and ginger, and sauté until fragrant.

5. Stir in broccoli, bell peppers, snap peas, and carrots. Stir-fry until the vegetables are tender-crisp.

6. In a small bowl, whisk together soy sauce or tamari.

7. Pour the sauce over the stir-fry and toss to coat.

8. Serve over cooked brown rice and garnish with sesame seeds and chopped green onions.

These high-protein organic vegan recipes are packed with delicious plant-based sources of protein and are perfect for maintaining a protein-rich diet. Enjoy these nutritious and satisfying meals!

Certainly! Here are 10 raw organic vegan recipes that are not only nutritious but also bursting with flavor:

Recipe 61: Raw Zucchini Noodles with Pesto

Ingredients:

- 4 organic zucchinis, spiralized into noodles

- 1 cup organic basil leaves

- 1/2 cup organic pine nuts

- 1/4 cup organic extra-virgin olive oil

- 2 cloves organic garlic

- Juice of 1 organic lemon

- Salt and pepper to taste

- Organic cherry tomatoes and extra basil leaves for garnish

Instructions:

1. In a food processor, combine basil, pine nuts, olive oil, garlic, lemon juice, salt, and pepper. Blend into a smooth pesto.

2. Toss the zucchini noodles with the pesto until well coated.

3. Garnish with cherry tomatoes and extra basil leaves before serving.

Recipe 62: Raw Rainbow Salad with Tahini Dressing

Ingredients:

- 2 cups organic red cabbage, thinly sliced

- 2 cups organic carrots, julienned

- 2 cups organic bell peppers (assorted colors), thinly sliced

- 2 cups organic broccoli florets

- 1 cup organic cherry tomatoes, halved
- 1/2 cup organic red onion, finely chopped
- 1/4 cup organic tahini
- Juice of 1 organic lemon
- 2 cloves organic garlic, minced
- 2 tbsp organic olive oil
- 2 tsp organic maple syrup
- Salt and pepper to taste
Instructions:
1. In a large bowl, combine red cabbage, carrots, bell peppers, broccoli, cherry tomatoes, and red onion.
2. In a small bowl, whisk together tahini, lemon juice, garlic, olive oil, maple syrup, salt, and pepper.
3. Drizzle the dressing over the salad and toss to combine.
Recipe 63: Raw Vegan Sushi Rolls
Ingredients:
- Nori seaweed sheets
- 2 cups organic cauliflower, finely grated
- 1 cup organic carrots, julienned
- 1 cup organic cucumber, julienned
- 1 cup organic bell peppers (assorted colors), julienned
- Organic avocado slices
- Organic alfalfa sprouts
- Organic pickled ginger
- Organic wasabi
- Organic soy sauce or tamari
Instructions:
1. Lay a nori sheet on a bamboo sushi rolling mat.
2. Spread a layer of grated cauliflower over the nori sheet.
3. Add julienned carrots, cucumber, bell peppers, avocado slices, and alfalfa sprouts.
4. Roll the nori sheet tightly using the bamboo mat.

5. Slice the roll into bite-sized pieces.

6. Serve with pickled ginger, wasabi, and soy sauce or tamari.

Recipe 64: Raw Vegan Stuffed Bell Peppers

Ingredients:

- 4 large organic bell peppers

- 2 cups organic cauliflower rice

- 1 cup organic cherry tomatoes, quartered

- 1/2 cup organic red onion, finely chopped

- 1/4 cup organic fresh basil, chopped

- 1/4 cup organic extra-virgin olive oil

- Juice of 1 organic lemon

- 2 cloves organic garlic, minced

- Salt and pepper to taste

Instructions:

1. Cut the tops off the bell peppers and remove the seeds.

2. In a large bowl, combine cauliflower rice, cherry tomatoes, red onion, basil, olive oil, lemon juice, garlic, salt, and pepper.

3. Stuff the bell peppers with the mixture.

4. Serve immediately or refrigerate for a refreshing and raw stuffed bell pepper.

Recipe 65: Raw Vegan Cucumber Gazpacho

Ingredients:

- 4 organic cucumbers, peeled and chopped

- 2 cups organic tomatoes, chopped

- 1/2 cup organic red onion, finely chopped

- 2 cloves organic garlic, minced

- 1/4 cup organic extra-virgin olive oil

- 2 tbsp organic red wine vinegar

- 1/4 cup organic fresh basil, chopped

- Salt and pepper to taste

Instructions:

1. In a blender, combine cucumbers, tomatoes, red onion, garlic, olive oil, red wine vinegar, basil, salt, and pepper.

2. Blend until smooth and chilled.

3. Serve this refreshing cucumber gazpacho cold.

Recipe 66: Raw Vegan Collard Green Wraps

Ingredients:

- Large organic collard green leaves
- 2 cups organic hummus
- 1 cup organic bell peppers (assorted colors), julienned
- 1 cup organic cucumber, julienned
- 1 cup organic carrots, julienned
- 1 cup organic avocado, sliced
- 1/4 cup organic sunflower seeds
- 1/4 cup organic alfalfa sprouts
- Organic tahini or your favorite dipping sauce

Instructions:

1. Lay a collard green leaf flat and spread a layer of hummus on it.

2. Add julienned bell peppers, cucumber, carrots, avocado slices, sunflower seeds, and alfalfa sprouts.

3. Roll the collard green leaf like a burrito, tucking in the sides as you go.

4. Slice in half and serve with tahini or your preferred dipping sauce.

Recipe 67: Raw Vegan Chia Pudding

Ingredients:

- 1/4 cup organic chia seeds
- 1 cup organic almond milk or coconut milk
- 1 tbsp organic maple syrup or agave nectar
- 1/2 tsp organic vanilla extract
- Organic fresh berries for topping

Instructions:

1. In a jar, combine chia seeds, almond milk or coconut milk, maple syrup or agave nectar, and vanilla extract.

2. Stir well to combine, then cover and refrigerate for at least 2 hours or overnight.

3. Top with fresh berries before serving.

Recipe 68: Raw Vegan Zucchini Tomato Salad

Ingredients:

- 3 organic zucchinis, thinly sliced

- 2 cups organic cherry tomatoes, halved

- 1/2 cup organic red onion, finely chopped

- 1/4 cup organic fresh basil, chopped

- 1/4 cup organic extra-virgin olive oil

- Juice of 1 organic lemon

- Salt and pepper to taste

Instructions:

1. In a large bowl, combine zucchini slices, cherry tomatoes, red onion, and basil.

2. In a small bowl, whisk together olive oil, lemon juice, salt, and pepper.

3. Drizzle the dressing over the salad and toss to combine.

Recipe 69: Raw Vegan Salsa

Ingredients:

- 2 cups organic tomatoes, diced

- 1/2 cup organic red onion, finely chopped

- 1/4 cup organic cilantro, chopped

- 2 cloves organic

garlic, minced

- Juice of 1 organic lime

- 1 organic jalapeño pepper, seeded and finely chopped (adjust to your spice preference)

- Salt and pepper to taste

Instructions:

1. In a bowl, combine tomatoes, red onion, cilantro, garlic, lime juice, jalapeño pepper, salt, and pepper.

2. Mix well and let the flavors meld for about 30 minutes before serving.

Recipe 70: Raw Vegan Nut and Seed Energy Bars

Ingredients:

- 1 cup organic dates, pitted
- 1/2 cup organic almonds
- 1/2 cup organic cashews
- 1/4 cup organic sunflower seeds
- 1/4 cup organic pumpkin seeds
- 1/4 cup organic chia seeds
- 1/4 cup organic shredded coconut
- 1/4 cup organic cacao powder
- 1 tsp organic vanilla extract
- A pinch of salt

Instructions:

1. In a food processor, combine dates, almonds, cashews, sunflower seeds, pumpkin seeds, chia seeds, shredded coconut, cacao powder, vanilla extract, and a pinch of salt.

2. Process until the mixture sticks together and forms a dough-like consistency.

3. Press the mixture into a square or rectangular pan lined with parchment paper.

4. Refrigerate until firm, then cut into bars.

These raw organic vegan recipes are not only healthy but also packed with vibrant flavors and nutrients. Enjoy the freshness of raw foods in these delicious dishes!

Certainly! Here are 10 quick and delicious organic vegan snack recipes to keep you satisfied throughout the day:

Recipe 71: Vegan Guacamole with Veggie Sticks

Ingredients:

- 2 organic avocados
- Juice of 1 organic lime

- 2 cloves organic garlic, minced
- 1/4 cup organic red onion, finely chopped
- 1 organic tomato, diced
- 1/4 cup organic cilantro, chopped
- Salt and pepper to taste
- Organic carrot, cucumber, and bell pepper sticks for dipping
Instructions:
1. Mash avocados in a bowl and mix in lime juice, garlic, red onion, tomato, and cilantro.
2. Season with salt and pepper.
3. Serve with carrot, cucumber, and bell pepper sticks for dipping.
Recipe 72: Vegan Peanut Butter and Banana Toast
Ingredients:
- 2 slices of your favorite organic whole-grain bread
- 2 tbsp organic peanut butter
- 1 organic banana, sliced
- Drizzle of organic agave nectar or maple syrup (optional)
Instructions:
1. Toast the bread until golden brown.
2. Spread peanut butter on the toasted slices.
3. Top with banana slices.
4. Drizzle with agave nectar or maple syrup if desired.
Recipe 73: Vegan Hummus and Veggie Wraps
Ingredients:
- Organic whole-grain or spinach tortillas
- 1 cup organic hummus
- Organic baby spinach leaves
- Organic bell peppers, thinly sliced
- Organic cucumbers, thinly sliced
- Organic carrots, julienned
Instructions:
1. Lay out a tortilla and spread a generous layer of hummus on it.

2. Add a handful of baby spinach leaves.

3. Top with sliced bell peppers, cucumbers, and julienned carrots.

4. Roll up the tortilla and cut it into bite-sized pieces for a convenient snack.

Recipe 74: Vegan Chia Pudding Parfait

Ingredients:

- 1/4 cup organic chia seeds

- 1 cup organic almond milk or coconut milk

- 1 tbsp organic maple syrup or agave nectar

- 1/2 tsp organic vanilla extract

- Organic fresh berries

- Organic granola

Instructions:

1. In a jar, combine chia seeds, almond milk or coconut milk, maple syrup or agave nectar, and vanilla extract.

2. Stir well to combine, then cover and refrigerate for at least 2 hours or overnight.

3. In a glass, layer chia pudding with fresh berries and granola for a delightful parfait.

Recipe 75: Vegan Rice Cakes with Almond Butter and Berries

Ingredients:

- Organic rice cakes

- Organic almond butter

- Organic berries (strawberries, blueberries, raspberries, etc.)

Instructions:

1. Spread almond butter on rice cakes.

2. Top with fresh organic berries.

Recipe 76: Vegan Trail Mix

Ingredients:

- 1 cup organic mixed nuts (almonds, walnuts, cashews)

- 1/2 cup organic dried fruits (raisins, cranberries, apricots)

- 1/4 cup organic dark chocolate chips

- 1/4 cup organic pumpkin seeds
- 1/4 cup organic sunflower seeds
Instructions:
1. Mix all the ingredients in a bowl.
2. Portion into small snack bags for easy grab-and-go snacks.
Recipe 77: Vegan Cucumber and Hummus Bites
Ingredients:
- Organic cucumber slices
- Organic hummus
Instructions:
1. Slice cucumbers into rounds.
2. Top each cucumber slice with a dollop of hummus.
Recipe 78: Vegan Popcorn with Nutritional Yeast
Ingredients:
- Organic popcorn kernels
- 2 tbsp organic coconut oil
- Nutritional yeast
- Salt to taste
Instructions:
1. Pop the popcorn using coconut oil.
2. While warm, sprinkle with nutritional yeast and salt for a cheesy flavor.
Recipe 79: Vegan Energy Bites
Ingredients:
- 1 cup organic rolled oats
- 1/2 cup organic peanut butter
- 1/3 cup organic honey or maple syrup
- 1/2 cup organic ground flaxseed
- 1/2 cup organic chocolate chips
- 1 tsp organic vanilla extract
Instructions:

1. In a bowl, combine oats, peanut butter, honey or maple syrup, ground flaxseed, chocolate chips, and vanilla extract.

2. Form the mixture into bite-sized energy balls.

3. Chill in the refrigerator for 30 minutes before enjoying.

Recipe 80: Vegan Sliced Apple and Almond Butter

Ingredients:

- Organic apple slices

- Organic almond butter

Instructions:

1. Slice an apple into wedges.

2. Dip the apple slices into almond butter for a crunchy and satisfying snack.

These quick and easy organic vegan snacks are perfect for satisfying your cravings and keeping you energized throughout the day. Enjoy the simplicity and deliciousness of these recipes!

Certainly! Here are 10 versatile organic vegan recipes that can be enjoyed for both breakfast and dessert:

Recipe 81: Vegan Banana Berry Smoothie Bowl

Ingredients:

- 2 ripe organic bananas, frozen

- 1 cup organic mixed berries (strawberries, blueberries, raspberries)

- 1/2 cup organic almond milk or coconut milk

- 2 tbsp organic chia seeds

- Toppings: Sliced organic banana, fresh berries, shredded coconut, and granola

Instructions:

1. Blend frozen bananas, mixed berries, almond milk, and chia seeds until smooth.

2. Pour the smoothie into a bowl.

3. Top with sliced banana, fresh berries, shredded coconut, and granola.

Recipe 82: Vegan Chia Pudding with Mango

Ingredients:
- 1/4 cup organic chia seeds
- 1 cup organic coconut milk
- 1 ripe organic mango, diced
- 1 tbsp organic maple syrup or agave nectar
- Organic shredded coconut and mint leaves for garnish
Instructions:

1. In a jar, combine chia seeds and coconut milk. Stir well and refrigerate for at least 2 hours or overnight.

2. Layer the chia pudding with diced mango.

3. Drizzle with maple syrup or agave nectar.

4. Garnish with shredded coconut and mint leaves.

Recipe 83: Vegan Chocolate Avocado Mousse

Ingredients:
- 2 ripe organic avocados
- 1/4 cup organic cocoa powder
- 1/4 cup organic maple syrup
- 1 tsp organic vanilla extract
- A pinch of salt
- Fresh organic berries for topping
Instructions:

1. Blend avocados, cocoa powder, maple syrup, vanilla extract, and a pinch of salt until smooth and creamy.

2. Serve the chocolate avocado mousse topped with fresh organic berries.

Recipe 84: Vegan Overnight Oats with Almond Butter

Ingredients:
- 1 cup organic rolled oats
- 1 cup organic almond milk
- 1 tbsp organic almond butter
- 1 tbsp organic maple syrup or agave nectar
- 1/2 tsp organic vanilla extract

- Sliced organic bananas for topping

Instructions:

1. In a jar, combine rolled oats, almond milk, almond butter, maple syrup, and vanilla extract.

2. Stir well, cover, and refrigerate overnight.

3. Top with sliced bananas before serving.

Recipe 85: Vegan Cinnamon Baked Apples

Ingredients:

- 2 organic apples, cored and halved

- 2 tbsp organic almond butter

- 1 tsp organic cinnamon

- 1 tbsp organic maple syrup or agave nectar

- Organic chopped nuts for garnish (e.g., almonds, walnuts)

Instructions:

1. Preheat the oven to 350°F (175°C).

2. In a small bowl, mix almond butter, cinnamon, and maple syrup.

3. Fill each apple half with the almond butter mixture.

4. Place the filled apple halves in a baking dish and bake for 20-25 minutes or until apples are tender.

5. Garnish with chopped nuts and serve warm.

Recipe 86: Vegan Coconut Chia Parfait

Ingredients:

- 1/4 cup organic chia seeds

- 1 cup organic coconut milk

- 1/2 cup organic mango, diced

- 1/4 cup organic granola

- Organic shredded coconut and fresh mint leaves for garnish

Instructions:

1. In a jar, combine chia seeds and coconut milk. Stir well and refrigerate for at least 2 hours or overnight.

2. Layer the chia pudding with diced mango.

3. Top with granola, shredded coconut, and fresh mint leaves.

Recipe 87: Vegan Mixed Berry Parfait

Ingredients:

- 1 cup organic mixed berries (strawberries, blueberries, raspberries)
- 1 cup organic coconut yogurt or almond yogurt
- 1/4 cup organic granola
- Organic fresh mint leaves for garnish

Instructions:

1. In a glass, layer mixed berries, coconut yogurt, and granola.

2. Garnish with fresh mint leaves.

Recipe 88: Vegan Raspberry Chia Jam

Ingredients:

- 2 cups organic raspberries
- 2 tbsp organic chia seeds
- 1 tbsp organic maple syrup
- 1/2 tsp organic lemon zest

Instructions:

1. In a saucepan, combine raspberries, chia seeds, maple syrup, and lemon zest.

2. Cook over low heat, stirring, until the raspberries break down and the mixture thickens (about 10 minutes).

3. Allow the jam to cool before using it as a topping for yogurt, oatmeal, or toast.

Recipe 89: Vegan Pumpkin Pie Smoothie

Ingredients:

- 1 cup organic pumpkin puree
- 1 cup organic almond milk
- 1 organic banana
- 1 tsp organic pumpkin pie spice
- 1 tbsp organic maple syrup
- Organic granola and ground cinnamon for topping

Instructions:

1. Blend pumpkin puree, almond milk, banana, pumpkin pie spice, and maple syrup until smooth.

2. Pour the smoothie into a glass and top with granola and a sprinkle of ground cinnamon.

Recipe 90: Vegan Chocolate Quinoa Bowl

Ingredients:

- 1 cup cooked organic quinoa

- 2 tbsp organic cocoa powder

- 1 tbsp organic maple syrup

- 1/2 cup organic almond milk

- Organic sliced strawberries and chopped nuts for topping

Instructions:

1. In a bowl, mix cooked quinoa, cocoa powder, maple syrup, and almond milk.

2. Top with sliced strawberries and chopped nuts for a satisfying breakfast or dessert bowl.

These organic vegan recipes can be enjoyed both for breakfast and dessert, offering a range of flavors from fruity to chocolaty to satisfy your cravings at any time of the day. Enjoy the versatility of these delicious dishes!

As you reach the end of this book, I want to leave you with a sweet and loving message, one that encapsulates the essence of your journey and the incredible transformation that's within your reach.

You've embarked on a remarkable path, one that's led you through the pages of "Thriving on Plants: The Ultimate Guide to an Organic Vegan Lifestyle." Along the way, you've discovered the profound impact of whole foods, the healing power of an organic vegan diet, and the joy of nurturing your body with nature's bounty.

Your journey has been shaped by knowledge, experience, and the understanding that our choices, both big and small, can have a profound impact not only on our own lives but on the world around us. You've embraced the importance of soil health, nutrient-dense foods, and the vibrant, colorful array of plant-based ingredients that Mother Nature has provided.

You've explored the stories of athletes like Novak Djokovic, vegan bodybuilders, and individuals who have defied the odds to live long, healthy lives fueled by the power of plants. You've delved into the magic of antioxidants, the wonders of gut health, and the delicious recipes that have graced these pages.

Now, as we stand at the precipice of new beginnings, I encourage you to take the next step on your journey—a journey towards the Ultimate Lifestyle Transformation. It's a 90-day commitment to yourself, a pledge to prioritize your well-being, to savor each meal as a celebration of life, and to embrace the incredible potential that exists within you.

With the knowledge and recipes you've discovered here, you hold the key to unlock a life filled with vitality, health, and joy. This is your time, your moment to shine, and your opportunity to thrive on plants. As you step into this new chapter of your life, remember that every day is a chance to nourish your body, to revitalize your spirit, and to inspire those around you.

The journey you've embarked upon is not just a lifestyle change; it's a testament to the love and care you have for yourself and for the world. You are a beacon of light, a force for positive change, and a living testament to the incredible transformation that's possible when we choose to thrive on plants.

With love and gratitude,

Kevin Luna

Certainly! Here's an inspirational message to motivate someone to embark on a 90-day Ultimate Lifestyle Transformation:

—-

◇ **Embark on Your 90-Day Ultimate Lifestyle Transformation** ◇

Dear Friend,

Life is a precious gift, a journey filled with countless opportunities to grow, to flourish, and to become the best version of ourselves. It's a canvas upon which we can paint our dreams, and a story we have the power to shape.

You may be standing at a crossroads, pondering the path to take. The 90-Day Ultimate Lifestyle Transformation isn't just a choice; it's a declaration of your commitment to a life that radiates health, vitality, and purpose. It's a journey to reconnect with the very essence of your being, to discover your potential, and to embrace a life that's aligned with your deepest values.

In the next 90 days, you can transform not only your body but your entire existence. You can awaken each day with a renewed sense of energy, a zest for life that invigorates every step you take. You can witness the incredible resilience of your body, the power of your mind, and the boundless love that flows from your heart.

As you embrace the Ultimate Lifestyle Transformation, you're not just nourishing your body; you're nurturing your spirit. You're making choices that resonate with the world around you, choices that are a testament to your love for yourself and your love for the planet we call home.

Imagine a life where you bound out of bed, ready to seize the day, your body humming with vitality. Imagine savoring every meal as an opportunity to celebrate the beauty of nature, to honor the Earth's abundance, and to fuel your potential. Imagine the impact of your journey, the ripple effect that spreads positivity, health, and inspiration to those you encounter.

This transformation isn't just about what you'll lose; it's about all that you'll gain. It's about the moments you'll cherish, the strength you'll uncover, and the joy that will become your constant companion. It's about becoming the best version of yourself and sharing that radiant energy with the world.

So, why should you embark on this 90-day journey? Because you deserve to experience the fullness of life. Because you have the power to transform not only your own world but the world at large. Because within you lies an untapped wellspring of potential waiting to burst forth.

Are you ready to take that first step? Are you ready to make the next 90 days a testament to your own greatness? Your transformation begins now, and it's a journey of love, self-discovery, and the celebration of life itself.

With unwavering belief in your journey,

Kevin Luna